Anxiety

A Workbook That Teaches You How To Quit Stressing Out About Money, Take Charge Of Your Financial Situation, And Enjoy A Happier Life

(Social Phobias In Order To Achieve Success In Any And Every Social Circumstance)

Michail Sigalas

TABLE OF CONTENT

The repercussions of what had occurred 1

Recognizing the Factors That Contribute to Your Anxiety 8

Acquiring Knowledge of the Amygdala 31

Managing Your Way Through the ACT 38

What are you going to do? Put your thoughts and feelings in writing 46

The Benefits That Come From Observing Other People 57

Taking Control of Your Depression 63

Think About Whether Or Not You Should Speak Out 80

The Primary Distinctions That Can Be Made Between Moods and Emotions 91

The Step-by-Step Guide to Starting a Conversation 98

Modify Your Way of Life to Be More Healthful. 116

Maintain a balance in your energy 121

The repercussions of what had occurred

Describe the effects that were brought about as a result of the activating event. At this point, it is best to ignore your ideas and concentrate instead on writing down your sentiments and how they made you feel. How strong, on a scale from zero to one hundred, would you say the emotion or feeling was? 0 indicates the lowest possible score, and 100 indicates the best possible score. Choose the one sensation or feeling that is most prominent in your mind in relation to what occurred, and emphasize that. Take notes on any behaviors or activities in which you took part or in which you engaged while the event was taking place, if any.

In addition to that, jot down some information regarding the responses that other people who were there gave to the occurrence. Did you get the impression that folks were helpful, annoyed, or indifferent? Did someone try to provoke you into an argument or make you feel even more self-conscious about your anxiety disorder? This will assist you in determining whether or not the group of people with whom you are spending your time is genuinely comprised of the kind of people in whom you would like to invest.

Your thoughts and ideas regarding the occurrence

Describe the beliefs you have regarding the occurrence of the incident. This could include one's thoughts, attitudes, expectations, or views. Put in writing whatever it was that you were considering at the moment, whatever was going through your thoughts at the time. Consider what is beyond the surface of such ideas by delving a little deeper into the topic. Put it in the form of a question: "What does that say about me?" or "and this is bad, because?" You need to continue digging until you can pinpoint the one notion that is giving you the greatest trouble. It should be underlined, and the degree to which you believe it should be rated on a scale from 0 to 100.

As you can see, a lot of these particulars require some level of involvement on your part. It is highly recommended that you return to your thought record at least twice for the purpose of taking notes. The first time should be just after the occurrence, while everything is still fresh in your memory and you may record your instant reaction. The second time should be some time later, after your mind has had more time to analyze the event and may be able to perceive the issue with greater clarity. It is possible that you will be shocked by how much insight this provides into the central problem.

Your unproductive patterns of thought

Describe any thought patterns that you may have had in the past that were counterproductive in terms of their connection to your beliefs. Mental filtering, thinking exclusively in black and white, leaping hastily to conclusions, overgeneralizing the problem, making it out to be a catastrophe, personalizing it, labeling, magnifying, and reducing are all examples of unproductive thought processes.

That one thought of yours that isn't helpful

Examine the notion that you highlighted as being the most detrimental to your progress earlier on. The ability to challenge the thoughts that you have is the actual key to being able to modify the mental patterns that you have been conditioned to have. Take into consideration the evidence that exists, both in support of and in opposition to that one concept, that one view that shines out above all the others. How practical is that line of thinking? What would have happened in that situation if you hadn't been plagued with anxiety? Is there something that you're overlooking, or is there another explanation possible? Consider how a different person might view the circumstance and how they would respond to it if they were in your shoes. Try to maintain a level of objectivity regarding the thoughts you have.

Changing one's mind about it

Last but not least, taking what you've learned in the preceding section, jot down some alternative thoughts, thoughts that are more balanced, thoughts that can replace that harmful one and change the direction the situation is headed in. The next step is to reevaluate the feeling that you connect most strongly with the occurrence and give it a rating. After that, evaluate the degree to which you still believe the harmful thought that you started with.

This phase is likely the most important of the whole process. If you just get rid of the problematic thoughts without replacing them with something constructive, there is a good probability that another unhelpful thought will fill the void left by the previous one. After you have compiled a comprehensive list of healthy, positive thoughts that can serve as replacements for unhealthy thoughts, make it a habit to regularly review this list. You can even choose to commit the list to memory if you so desire. When you find yourself in a scenario where negative ideas are beginning to emerge, this will enable you to have a positive thought to fall back on instantly so that you can combat those bad thoughts.

Recognizing the Factors That Contribute to Your Anxiety

In most cases, an external factor is what initially causes anxiety in a romantic partnership. It's possible that it's connected to the fact that you and your partner argue all the time, that you don't trust each other, or that you have low self-esteem. After determining the source of your nervous feelings, the next step is to address the most significant aspect of the issue at hand.

There are some people who may have the perception that their lover is simply unattainable for them. If you fall into this group, you'll find that you frequently find yourself thinking things like, "He's too handsome, he's too intelligent, he's too generous," or any one of a number of other traits that make you feel as though your partner is just too good for you to want to be with them. These feelings can lead to feelings of insecurity, and before you know it, you could find yourself caught in a vicious cycle of panic.

When you have low self-esteem, you will start to feel as though you are not worthy of or do not deserve the affection of your partner. When this happens, you start to worry that they are going to stop working with you or find someone else to take your place. This begins to stoke your fear of being abandoned, and as a result, you find yourself obsessing over the state of your relationships on a continual basis. Anxiety is triggered not by things happening in the outside world for persons like this, but by things happening within themselves.

When the source of your hysteria is found within yourself, it is typically more difficult to settle the issue because there is nothing that your partner can do to reassure you. You will never be able to stop worrying that you are unworthy of love until you are prepared to establish a healthy sense of self-esteem. If poor self-esteem or feelings of unworthiness are what cause your anxiety, the first step toward recovery is to become attentive of the ideas that run through your head.

In intimate relationships, a lack of trust can be an everyday source of anxiety. As soon as you have any reason to doubt the motives of your partner, you will automatically begin to assume the worst. Because of this fear, the dynamic in the relationship shifts to one in which you are always on the offensive, and your spouse frequently finds themselves in the position of having to defend themselves.

A lack of trust may also be the result of previous negative experiences or of anything that your partner has done that has caused you to question their reliability. If the actions you are taking are not addressing the lack of trust, then worry will take over because you will not know how the relationship will develop in the future.

If the lack of trust in your relationship is the source of your relationship anxiety, you will feel the need to keep a close eye on what your partner is doing all the time. You'll find yourself looking through their phones or coming up with reasons to visit them at their place of employment if you don't stop. When they are speaking to another person on the phone, you will start to feel anxious. It's possible that living with you will become a living nightmare because of your paranoia. It gives the impression that the other person is imprisoned and makes them feel as though they are trapped.

Trust problems are a surefire way to ruin a relationship. The problem with anxiety is that your trust concerns aren't always rational or built on facts. This is one of the things that causes it. To fit the story that you've concocted in your head, you'll simply be imagining things or exaggerating the significance of innocuous happenings beyond all reasonable bounds. One of the most effective strategies for causing a partner to leave you is to constantly wonder and distrust what they are doing.

You will find that it is easier to keep your anxiety under control if you are aware of the factors that exacerbate your trust problems. Instead of bottling up your feelings and allowing them to fester, talk to your significant other about the things that make you feel insecure. Make it known to them that there are some actions on their part that cause you to have less faith in them. For instance, if your spouse is someone who is prone to flirting with other people, you should let them know that it makes you feel nervous when you see them engaging in such behavior with other people.

It may be challenging to be upfront about your worries, but doing so is essential since it is the only way to address the problem that is causing your worry. When you begin to feel that it is necessary to continually monitor the lives of your partner, it is a sign that your worry is getting the better of you. It is much more effective to create trust through open dialogue than it is to seek reassurance through covert surveillance.

Another typical kind of anxiety that can be brought on by relationships is jealousy. Jealousy is often the result of a combination of low self-esteem and an inability to trust others. When you repeatedly compare yourself to others, you set yourself up for a lifelong battle against the emotion of envy. It's possible that your partner has acquaintances or coworkers that you consider to be more accomplished than you, in some way or another. Because of this, you find yourself feeling envious of them and viewing them as a threat to the relationship.

When you allow jealousy to fuel your worry in a relationship, you will begin to be possessive and clinging toward the other person. You feel as though it is unacceptable for your partner to have interests or activities outside of the relationship. You have the incorrect idea that the best way to protect your partner from other people is to isolate yourself and your partner from the rest of the world by spending all of your time with each other. Jealousy is the single most effective way to end a relationship quickly.

In the same way that low self-esteem is an internal source of tension, jealousy is an internal source of stress, and there is nothing that your partner or anyone else can do to alleviate your uneasiness. It takes enough popularity for you to simply have an unhealthy idea of who you are before you can begin to get over your jealousy. When it comes to relationships, jealousy is one of the most toxic feelings that may arise. Jealousy can lead to aggressive and violent behavior because, in most situations, the person experiencing it feels the need to protect their territory in order to guard against the perceived threat from the outside world.

Learn to read the signs your behavior is giving you to determine the source of your worry. It is likely that you are experiencing envy if you do not want your boyfriend to interact with other people out of the fear that he would eventually leave you for those other individuals.

Insecurities of a fleeting kind are natural in romantic partnerships, and the vast majority of people will, at some point, feel jealousy in the course of their romantic lives. Jealousy can be considered pathological, though, if it causes you to continually fear that other people are better than you or that they will steal your relationship from you.

Another prevalent factor that can bring on anxious feelings in romantic partnerships is chronic stress. Some romantic partnerships are perpetually fraught with tension and anxiety for both parties involved. These are the unhealthy kinds of partnerships in which there is little to no harmony between the two people involved. Included in this category are codependent relationships, partnerships characterized by narcissistic manipulation, as well as abusive relationships. It should come as no surprise that this kind of stress leads to anxiety in your relationship because it is a common denominator in the kinds of relationships that are experiencing it.

For instance, if you suffer from codependence, you are constantly preoccupied with concerns regarding the other person. Is he content, what does he want me to do, did I provide adequate support, am I letting him down, and what can I do to make him happy? Because you have an intrinsic desire to find a way to make the other person happy, these questions are always running through your head. since of this, you are in a constant state of worry about the condition of your relationship with them since you are preoccupied with their requirements.

Anxiety is a constant companion in unhealthy relationships because there is no foundation upon which to build a sense of safety and stability. You are keenly aware that everything can fail at any time, regardless of the circumstances. You have the impression that you are helpless to leave the relationship, despite the fact that you are miserable there. Toxic relationships can easily set off significant anxiety, which can then create a variety of health problems, including inability to sleep, elevated vital signs, and even gastrointestinal diseases.

If your anxiety is being triggered by a relationship that is difficult or poisonous for you, the best solution is sometimes to quit the relationship. Keeping toxic connections in your life implies that you have to deal with anxiety on a day-to-day level. If your anxiety persists for an extended period of time, it will start to have an impact on your mental state, your capacity to operate properly, and even your social life.

This book contains information that can be put into action and teaches readers how to study individuals and develop a deeper understanding of the human mind in order to cultivate success, master skills, and build healthy relationships. Almost everyone has found themselves in a situation, either in their personal lives or in their professional lives, when they wished they could better comprehend other people. We are curious in the mental state of our partners, friends, parents, children, siblings, and any other relatives with whom we are interacting at the moment. Is he or she even interested in us? Is the individual open to our ideas and recommendations? Is he or she confident in our abilities? Is he or she faking their affection for us when the reality is that they do not? The same holds true in professional contexts; we want to know whether our interviewer likes us, whether a prospective customer loves our pitch or is disinterested, whether a colleague is lying to us or not, whether our boss likes us, and a great deal more besides. It doesn't end there; we even want to know what the person standing next to us on the street is thinking, as well as what the person sitting next to us on the bus, train, movie theater, etc. thinks of us, whether he or she is interested in us, and so on. It would be amazing if we could just cut to the chase and know what other people are thinking or doing, even if they are unaware that they are talking with us. All of this, however, falls under the purview of psychology, which is concerned with gaining an understanding of the human mind. This is the perfect book for you if you are interested in cultivating genuine, long-lasting relationships and want to focus your efforts on the relationships and people in your life that truly matter. It will teach you how to "read" people as if they were an open book, which is essential for achieving the aforementioned goals. This has nothing to do with having superpowers, so you don't need to worry about that; rather, it has everything to do with understanding humans on a level that enables you to evaluate individuals with a great deal of ease. That's what you should be concerned about.

In this book, you will begin to discover how to comprehend what piques their interests, what infuriates them, their belief system, their perceptions, and much more that you need to be aware of in order to use that to your advantage if you want to use that to use that to your advantage. You should be able to 'decode' literally anyone if you read this book and follow everything in it to the letter.

Here is a Sample of the Information That You Will Acquire...

Analyzing and comprehending people's mental states requires consideration of a number of factors.

Interpreting a Person Based on Their Body Language

Conducting an Analysis of People's Conversations and Speaking Patterns

Conducting an Analysis of People's Conversations and Speaking Patterns

Taking Notice of People's Routines in Addition to a Great Deal More!

Now comes the difficult portion of the process. Now, in addition to reading a book on how to deal with your anxiety and get through it, you have additional responsibilities. Anxiety affects not just the mind but also the body. At this point, you are going to need to take active steps to conquer your anxiety. You have been provided with sufficient resources to assist you in effectively stepping out of your mental box, including information about the type of anxiety you experience and how it manifests itself, as well as coping methods and the lists you have typed down. This week, you will be able to arrange your lists, come up with game plans to handle situations that increase worry, and make attempts to face both a real trigger of yours and an assumed trigger of yours. The following is a list of activities that you should do each day as part of the challenges that will be presented to you over the course of the next thirty days:

- Achieve the daily objective you set for yourself.
- Determine a target for the upcoming week.
- Engage in physical activity and/or a method of mental or physical relaxation such as yoga or meditation.
- Keep a journal tracking your anxiety levels as well as your improvements.
- Write down the things for which you are thankful in a journal.

It seems possible, doesn't it? Absolutely, this is the case. This week, you will have the ability to ease into it, and by the end of the month, you should aim to make it as much of a habit as possible. Following the completion of your 30-day challenge, you will have an increased chance of being able to effectively maintain this habit.

Day One: Let's get started with some sense of direction today. Take a look at the list of issues that need to be fixed that you have created. If there is anything that you have identified as a problem that contributes further to your anxiety, use that problem as the focus of your weekly goal that you intend to achieve for yourself and make it a priority. Create a written outline of the steps that need to be taken in order to achieve your goal. Make a plan for yourself of actionable tasks that you can picture yourself completing in no more than seven days, regardless of whether it is a significant task that you have been putting off for a long time or something more straightforward, such as cleaning the clutter out of a specific room or your entire house. If it is something more essential, such as a legal duty or something connected to your employment, you should make it a goal to at least make a dent in the amount of effort that will be required to do it. It is crucial to assess your level of anxiety at the beginning of the day and again after you have completed each of these actions throughout the day or week. Rate your degree of anxiety on a scale that ranges from one, which indicates that you have no anxiety at all, to ten, which indicates that you are very close to having a panic or anxiety attack. This will allow you to evaluate how much progress is achieved after you perform these actions. When you finally finish your assignment and realize your objective, you are likely to feel a sense of relief. As a result of this, you will be able to benefit from experiencing fewer levels of anxiety as a result.

Day Two: When you woke up this morning, make a mental note of the time, and make it a goal to get up at the same time every morning for at least the next thirty days, if not longer. Examine the to-do list you produced in order to achieve the weekly objective you set for yourself. Set the next item on that list as your daily objective, and work toward completing it.

You should try a more upbeat activity if you were not as effective as you had hoped to be in finishing the task you were given the day before. Verbalize the objective that you have set for yourself for this week in your brain. Declare out loud that you will achieve the task and the goal you have set for yourself, and that you will be successful. The same phrase should be repeated three to five times. You are providing your brain more mental power over the consequences that worry is trying to drag you down with by saying this, thus it is important that you do it. This is an example of thought over matter, and it has the potential to be quite successful.

When you repeat this sentence, you should do it with the full conviction that what you are stating is accurate. After you have completed this challenging mental exercise, you should attempt to go forward with your task and goal.

Choose a pastime that you enjoy doing in order to give yourself a chance to unwind and chill down today. Take in a movie or one of your favorite shows.

Day Three: Your mission for today is to introduce yourself to someone you don't know. The other person with whom you talked may not have been conversational, but at least they didn't start a scene or insult you, contrary to what your nervousness may have led you to believe would happen in such a situation. Perhaps the other person approached you first and struck up a discussion with you, which went swimmingly.

After a long day, you are going to want some time to relax and unwind. Try engaging in some calming activities like yoga for at least 15 to 20 minutes while playing soothing music. Pandora has a plethora of Zen music CDs, all of which are guaranteed to divert your attention elsewhere while you focus on achieving physical equilibrium and relaxation. Taking a shower or bath every day is never a terrible idea. Today, you should relax in a bath scented with your preferred essential oil.

Day Four: If decluttering your home or a specific space was one of the goals on your "Pesky Problems" list that contributed to your anxiety, make it your daily aim to concentrate on achieving this objective. whether you are still working toward your weekly goal but you aren't sure whether you have enough time to fully immerse yourself in this project, spend at least thirty minutes cleaning and doing whatever you can to reduce the amount of clutter in your living area. This will give you more time to focus on your weekly objective. There will be sufficient time to make some significant advancements. If you don't regularly make this a daily priority, adding 30 minutes of cleaning time to your daily routine will help you find an increasingly fewer number of things that need to be cleaned or cleared out.

A pen exercise is one type of activity that can help you boost the natural quantity of pleasant feelings you experience as well as your overall sense of happiness. This can be done pretty much anyplace there is a pen lying about. You just need to grab a pen and hold it between your upper and lower front teeth. While you are participating in this activity, smile so much that you can't even tell when your lips are touching the pen. Give it a shot for the next five minutes. In spite of the fact that you need to sterilize the pen, if you make an effort to grin for this length of time, you can convince your brain that you are content and that everything in your life is going swimmingly well. During the course of the day, you might find that you are smiling more frequently, which can take you a long way. Increasing the frequency with which you smile will lift your general disposition and enhance the likelihood that you will experience happy feelings rather than negative ones.

Acquiring Knowledge of the Amygdala

It is important to remember not to let the size of your amygdala fool you. Even though the cortex, the largest and most complicated part of the human brain, contributes to anxiety from multiple perspectives, the amygdala plays the most important role because, as you may recall from earlier, it is involved with both the amygdala pathway and the cortex pathway that leads to anxiety. The amygdala, analogous to the conductor of an orchestra, is in charge of a wide variety of responses in both the cerebrum and the rest of the body. It is also totally delicate to what befalls you and how it reacts to the specific experiences you have because it depends on reactions that have been preset.

Find out as soon as possible about the unique "language" spoken by the amygdala and the impact it has on your life. The amygdala is a very ancient structure in terms of its evolutionary history, and the amygdala of the human being is extremely similar to the amygdalae that are found in every single other organism. Because of its similarity to amygdalae found in rats, dogs, and even fish, scientists have been able to investigate the human amygdala in great detail and have learned a great deal about the processes that underlie the production of fear and anxiety.

Your amygdala is already programmed with responses when you are conceived, and these responses are ready to be employed in a variety of different contexts. However, this ancient structure isn't set in stone; the amygdala is always picking up new information and evolving based on the experiences you have on a day-to-day basis. When you get an understanding of what we refer to as "the language of the amygdala," you will have a greater degree of control over the ways in which you react to anxious situations. This is because you will know how to alter the region of the brain that is at the very core of dread.

AMYGDALA AS A GUARDIAN OR PROTECTOR

It is helpful to think of the amygdala as your protector in order to gain an understanding of the anxiety that is caused by the amygdala. People have an amygdala that generates fear and has the primary goal of surviving as its function as a result of natural selection. The amygdala keeps a vigilant eye out for anything that could indicate a risk of injury as you move closer to the start of your day. Even while the goal of insurance is commendable, the amygdala has the potential to go too far, causing a fear reaction in situations that aren't typically dangerous.

Take for example Fran, who is going to deliver a presentation. As she stands in front of the group with everyone's eyes on her, her palms begin to sweat as her heartbeat quickens. She also begins to hyperventilate. Why does her amygdala feel the need to protect her from whatever it is? It would indicate that it views the circumstance of having to stand in front of a number of people as being potentially dangerous. This kind of response is experienced by a lot of people, not just Fran. According to research conducted by Dwyer and Davidson (2012), the dread of public speaking is the most prevalent of all fears, ranking higher than the fear of flying, fear of insects, fear of heights, and fear of being confined in a small place. What could be considered a normal response to this situation? As a result of the amygdala's efforts to protect us from becoming prey to a dangerous animal, experts who study human development have hypothesized that we may have a tendency to interpret eyes watching us as a sign that we are in a potentially dangerous situation (Ohman 2007). Others have claimed that the dread of being dismissed by a group of observers derives from an ancient fear of being dismissed by one's tribe (Croston 2012). In the past, being dismissed by one's tribe meant being left all alone to fight for yourself and face wandering predators, which was essentially the same as being executed. In spite of this, it would appear that the human amygdala reacts to prevent us from being in the vulnerable position of being seen by potentially dangerous creatures, including other people.

It's possible that Fran is unaware of the developmental underpinnings that underlie her response and the role that the amygdala plays in it. While her brain may be revealing to her that she is concerned about being criticized, ashamed, or making a mistake, her amygdala may be operating from an increasingly archaic point of view. Her cortex may be revealing this to her. In point of fact, the brain is constantly contemplating the reasons for our behaviors, and these reasons could be very specific explanations. However, the issue at hand is not the precise nature of the cortex; rather, it is the characteristics of its constituents. The more that Fran ruminates on cortex-generated clarifications for her amygdala-based anxiety, for instance, she is anxious that her supervisor will not be happy with her introduction, the more cortex-based anxiety that she will make, which will add to her concern. Comparable to looking in the refrigerator to figure out why your car won't start, looking for the causes of amygdala-based anxiety in the cortex is like trying to find the cause of a stalled automobile. You haven't even begun to search in the right place!

Managing Your Way Through the ACT

The adventure that is life, similar to the odyssey you had on the ACT, is full of beginnings and endings, highs and lows, forward movement and regress. The following are four difficulties that individuals may run across while attempting to live an ACT lifestyle. Having this knowledge will assist prevent you from falling into a state of discouragement.

Lack of patience

If you have ever observed a preschooler learning how to tie their shoes, then you are familiar with the expression of impatience. Even when participating in acceptance and commitment treatment, some clients experience feelings of frustration and a sense that they are not progressing toward "the outcome" fast enough. Keep in mind, however, that the ACT is not a quick remedy for your issues; rather, it is an odyssey. It's a process similar to learning how to tie your shoes, so be patient. Your ability to practice patience with yourself will go a long way toward assisting you in the long-term development of a life that is motivated by your values.

Inexcusable Racing

Exciting times lie ahead as you embark on your journey to design and live a life of superior quality. However, there are occasions when people strive to move too quickly, and as a result, they create objectives for themselves that are unachievable in the near term. You will be able to take increasingly effective action as your trip progresses if you devote the necessary amount of time to learning about the ACT ideas and how to work with them, as well as if you carry out all of the activities contained in this book. You don't want to be like the kid who hastily wads up their shoelaces into a loose lump and then starts running, only to trip and fall when the shoelaces come undone because you don't want to be that kid.

A sense of reluctance

You don't want to set objectives and attempt actions that are unrealistically large for this point in your trip, but you also don't want your goals and actions to be so insignificant that you don't feel like you're making any headway at all. Even if you are confident that you are prepared for a different kind of life, making adjustments in your life can be challenging and frightening. What happens if the outcomes are not to your satisfaction? What if you don't succeed? These are unsettling issues, and often individuals try to avoid answering them by establishing goals that are either too simple or too modest to result in any kind of meaningful progression. Do you remember when you were a kid and you knew it was important for you to figure out how to tie your shoes? What would have occurred if you had simply put them away in the closet and considered the possibility of teaching yourself how to knot them someday? In order to avoid falling into the trap of indecision, you should never set a goal for yourself without first considering how successful completion of the objective will help you advance.

Strategies for Brain Training That Will Guarantee Unrivaled Concentration

Patience, determination, willpower, and mental clarity are all necessary components of concentration in an individual. By paying attention to everything and anything that is significant, focus ultimately enables a person to learn more effectively, perform more productively, and behave more intelligently.

Improving your ability to concentrate is always the ideal place to begin when it comes to the workouts that are designed to train your brain.

Methods for Increasing Your Capacity to Focus and Concentrate

Your ability to concentrate is going to prove to be very beneficial to your brain training in the long term. However, before we go into how to improve your focus, there is something extremely crucial that you need to realize first. If you are working too hard to concentrate, you are not concentrating.

Because concentration is a taught skill, the only way to acquire it is through constant practice using the appropriate techniques. This means that it can only be learnt. Even if your capacity to concentrate can be momentarily boosted while you are working on other projects by employing a variety of techniques, the results will not be as good as those you get from developing your ability to concentrate as a distinct endeavor.

Your capacity to ignore distractions that are stopping you from concentrating in the first place has an effect on both your ability to concentrate and your ability to ignore distractions.

You can try practicing the following exercises to acquire unprecedented levels of focus as well as to reap the advantages of doing so over the course of a longer period of time:

Counting backwards is one of the simplest and most straightforward exercises you can do to improve your concentration. In addition to that, it is a good way to get warmed up before beginning additional brain training exercises. To get started, count backwards from ten to one to get to one. After this, you should begin your countdown from twenty. Repeat the entire process, this time being sure to gradually increase your starting number to achieve the highest possible total. Make a note of your accomplishments in your personal journal and strive to achieve even better results during the subsequent workout.

Advanced (advanced) Counting Backwards is the activity that is a more difficult version of the one that came before it. Try skipping three numbers as you count backwards from 10. Start at ten and count backwards from there. For instance, count to ten, seven, four, one, and then twenty, seventeen, fourteen, eleven, nine, six, and zero. Continue to raise the first number until you have reached the maximum possible. Once more, make sure to write down your results in your own personal journal and strive to improve upon them in subsequent efforts.

Rapid Stimulation of the Senses You have the option to pay for professional sensory stimulation sessions such as massage, aromatherapy, music therapy, and other such services. However, you also have the option of performing a brief sensory stimulation exercise of your own devising at home. A person's sensory memory is the part of their brain that is in charge of processing information for a very little amount of time (less than one second). To begin the exercise, gather the following items: any music player (such as an iPod or a mobile phone), any flavored non-alcoholic drink (such as tea, hot chocolate, or lemonade), and any book. The next thing you need to do is look around your home for the most comfy chair you can locate and then sit in it. Make sure that you are seated in a position that allows you to access everything without having to get up from the chair. After this, make an effort to unwind and concentrate on enjoying a variety of activities at the same time. The final stage is to write down in your diary using brief phrases a description of each sensation you experienced (such as the flavor of the drink, the song that was playing, etc.).

Simple Exercises in Meditative Breathing -Simple meditation can be practiced anywhere and in any posture, in contrast to formal meditation, which typically involves sitting on a cushion and burning incense. First, close your eyes and picture a metallic container in your mind. Put whatever that comes to your mind in the box, then shut it. Do this for the next minute. After that, concentrate on the closed box for about five minutes, or until you reach a state of complete relaxation, whichever comes first.

Keep in mind that the optimum time to perform the exercises described above is when you have some free time on your hands, and not while you are concentrating on completing an essential project. Doing so will just divert your attention away from the aforementioned activity. It will take some practice to improve your concentration, but once you do, you will notice the difference almost immediately.

The exercises that are designed to improve your focus will each only take a few minutes of your time, making it simple to include them into your regular routine. Just keep in mind that you should document any progress you make in your notebook so that you can figure out which form of exercise benefits you the most.

Training for Mental Clarity and Concentration

Your capacity for attention, mental clarity, and focus are all contributing factors to your capacity for learning and having experiences that are constructive. Clearing your mind can help you improve the quality of what you learn as well as the quality of the work that you produce. While attention and focus can assist you in prioritizing the completion of intellectually taxing tasks, mental clarity can help you improve both.

What are you going to do? Put your thoughts and feelings in writing.

According to the findings of the study that came before this one, writing down your feelings on some paper may help your brain function more effectively. The use of this method releases the mind from its preoccupation with problems. When you worry too much, your mind will start to wander and become preoccupied.

When this occurs, it will be quite difficult for you to concentrate on what you're doing. Why? Because your brain is attempting to perform multiple things at once, including monitoring and repressing your fears. The primary author of the study, Hans Schroder, came to the following conclusion about the outcomes of the investigation: "Our findings show that if you get these worries out of your head through expressive writing, those cognitive resources are freed up to work toward the task you're completing and you become more efficient."

To put it another way, putting your thoughts and feelings into writing can assist your brain become more focused. Not only can writing about one's feelings help alleviate stress immediately, but it will also help the brain concentrate better while one is engaged in a difficult activity.

One of the other co-authors of the study thinks that writing freely about one's feelings can also assist the body get ready for any stressful activity that lies ahead. One of the researchers involved in the study, Dr. Jason Moser, came to the following conclusion on his own: "Expressive writing makes the mind work less hard on upcoming stressful tasks, which is what worriers often get "burned out" over, their worried minds working harder and hotter."

Try your hand at some expressive writing if you're the type of person who suffers from excessive worry. Spend a little bit of time writing down how you are currently feeling. It is very interesting to learn how simple it is to get rid of tension immediately. The benefits of utilizing this method include the fact that it is both speedy and uncomplicated.

12. Sit in quiet reflection.

Our thoughts tend to stray. Not only that, but it is also capable of anticipating the occurrence of certain events. But there is one issue, and that is that it can be overly dramatic at times. Exaggerated thoughts eventually manifest as concerns and worries, which lead to anxiety in the sufferer.

If this condition is not treated in the appropriate manner, it may lead to more serious mental health problems. Over the course of several decades, researchers in several fields of psychology have been looking for answers. And in the vast majority of cases, professionals rely significantly on medication and treatment in order to bring a disordered mind under control.

To combat your fears and anxiety, fortunately, you do not need to resort to medicine or spend a lot of money on expert services. A recent study discovered an easy and cost-effective method for controlling one's mental state. People who struggle with anxiety can benefit greatly from practicing mindfulness for ten minutes.

The mind can be trained to stop thinking about unimportant things through the simple practice of mindfulness. Additionally, it enables the mind to become more focused on the event that is happening right now. Mengran Xu, the primary author of the study, provided an explanation of the findings. According to

Xu, "We also found that regular meditation practice appears to help anxious people to shift their attention from their own internal worries to the present-moment external world, which enables better focus on a task that is currently being performed."

The use of mindfulness as a therapeutic method to alleviate fears and anxiety is not a recent development. The ancient people were the first to harness its power, which dates back several thousand years.

Researchers have just very lately discovered the enormous beneficial effects that this method has on the health of human beings. This method of self-improvement is advantageous in that it requires very little effort and can be carried out almost anyplace.

The Ultimate Guide to Meditation: How Can I Meditate at Home?

There is no doubt that meditation has a number of beneficial effects on one's health. Stress, depression, and various other psychological issues are alleviated as a result. Nevertheless, the procedure calls for an ideal setting. And that ideal location could very well be your own home. Yes, it is possible to meditate even inside, without getting into the fresh air.

The following is a guide that will walk you through each phase of the meditation process.

1. Go someplace calm and quiet.

A calm, private setting that allows you to focus is essential for successful meditation. It could be in the room you sleep in, the garage, or even the basement of your house. Any location that is devoid of background noise.

2. Place your legs over the floor in front of you and sit down.

It's likely that you've witnessed others doing meditation at some point. They all sit with their legs crossed on the floor in the same manner, which is a regular body position for them. Proceed in the same manner.

3. Maintain a proud posture.

Please maintain a calm and upright posture. Imagine that you are leaning against a wall that is completely flat.

4. Try to relax your entire body.

Put your hands over your eyes and begin to focus on how your body feels. You might choose to begin at your feet and work your way up to your head, starting at your ankles. You need to make sure that you are relaxing your entire body while you are doing this, so pay attention to this. Relax the muscles in your neck, tongue, and shoulders. This will help you breathe better.

5. Keep your calm.

Start paying attention to the sounds that are occurring in your environment now that you are feeling more at ease. Simply keep an eye on your immediate environment. But refrain from responding and instead simply silently listen. Do not let your mind come to any conclusions or draw any interpretations based on the sound that you are hearing. Please be aware of this.

6. Take a long, slow breath.

The next thing you should do when you are meditating is to concentrate on your breathing. Take calm, in-depth breaths as you speak. Do not force air into your lungs; simply fill them up. During the entire process of inhaling and exhaling, pay attention to the feeling that you get as air travels past your nose, throat, and chest.

7. Determine the appropriate time to conclude the practice.

When it comes to meditating, there is no set time restriction on how long the process should last for each individual. On the other hand, if you are just starting off, you should begin with a shorter amount of time. Perhaps between 5 and 10 minutes. However, as you level up, you will unlock the ability to extend the time limit. If you need to wake yourself up at a certain hour, you can use an alarm clock.

8. Devote some time each day to meditating.

How frequently should you make time to meditate? To be honest, there is no one correct solution to this problem. However, setting out at least five minutes each day to meditate can be both healthy and rewarding.

Meditation is the easiest approach to calm both your mind and your body at the same time. Not to mention the benefits it offers in the treatment of mental health conditions including stress, despair, and anxiety. First and foremost, there is no charge. Begin meditating right away to feel the positive, transformative effects it has on your health and well-being.

I really hope that by doing this exercise, we can assist you get rid of those fears. If there is a particular occurrence in your life that causes you anxiety, all you need to do is sit quietly and reflect for a while. You will benefit from it if you carry it out in the proper manner.

The Benefits That Come From Observing Other People

When it comes to being able to analyze other people, you have a number of crucial advantages that can help you, and there are also a number of scenarios in which you can utilize your ability to analyze other people to aid you in your own life. After you have gained the knowledge necessary to assess other individuals, you will be able to put that knowledge to use in the most effective manner imaginable. The more you make use of it, the greater the likelihood that you may discover a technique to completely improve the circumstance that you are now in. Consider it in this light: you can pause for a moment and think about the fact that you are reading the minds of individuals around you by looking at the behaviors they are performing. This is something that we have previously established beyond a reasonable doubt. Now, all that will be required of you is to guarantee that you are making the effort to realize the many ways in which this can be of advantage to you.

In this chapter, we will discuss many significant ways that you can use the ability to analyze others to help yourself in real-life settings. These are ways that you can use your ability to analyze others to help yourself. We will look at some important applications that can be of service to virtually anyone. Reading people is a skill that everyone ought to acquire, regardless of whether they are introverted, extroverted, interested in other people, or not interested in other people at all.

Improved Capacity to Negotiate
When you begin to negotiate with other individuals, you are working toward the

goal of reaching some kind of an agreement between the persons involved. You and another person are going to have a conversation in which you go through each step of the process of figuring out what it is that each of you wants and where the two of you have something in common. It's possible that what you want and what they want are two completely different things; in this case, you'll need to decide out which concessions you're willing to make. However, if neither you nor the other person is truly eager to cooperate with one another during the negotiation process, it will be impossible for either of you to ensure that things get off to a good start. Because of this, you will not be able to collaborate effectively with anyone who is involved. You may, however, learn how to better engage others by improving your ability to interpret their body language. This is something you can do.

Imagine the following: You are currently seated next to the other party, who gives the impression of not being particularly receptive to engaging in negotiation with you in the first place. Do you believe that you will make significant progress in this endeavor? It's possible that they are sitting there with their arms crossed and their back turned to you because they don't want to engage in the conversation. There is a good probability that they do not want to have anything to do with you at all, and because of this, they make every effort to avoid situations in which they would have to interact with you. They stopped using any sort of body language.

If you are able to recognize this quality in another person, you can deduce that they are not now willing to engage in that form of negotiation in the first place.

This indicates that the best course of action that you can take is to give yourself the necessary amount of time to pause and reflect. You will be able to convince yourself that you do not wish to deal with the situation, and as a result, you will not be as effective as you would be if they were more upfront with you. You are aware of this, but you are unable to move forward. In this particular scenario, the most beneficial action that you can take would be to make it a priority to identify ways in which you can participate more actively. When you've figured out the ideal way to communicate with the other person, you can start thinking about what it will take to get them to share more personal information with you.

When you are able to read the other person, you can then start to figure out how to engage in the conversation in the most productive way. You will learn what it will take for you to really talk to them and how to accomplish this goal. You will gain the knowledge necessary to interact with them in an appropriate manner. It is essential that you do this, as it will enable you to improve your overall satisfaction with the circumstances that currently exist. This is quite important, and you need to make certain that you are in a position in which you can engage more effectively. When you reach that stage, you are confident that you will be in a better position to negotiate once you get there. You have to figure out how to use your own body language to influence other people so that theirs will open up to you. You eventually succeed in making them more inclined to interact with you, and as a result, you are given the opportunity to negotiate.

Taking Control of Your Depression

The meaning of

There is a distinction between feeling sad and being depressed. It is a mental condition that can be recognized by a distinct collection of signs and symptoms that can be evaluated by a medical professional. When we are experiencing feelings of depression, our thoughts, feelings, and behaviors all work together to make us feel worse. If you are experiencing feelings of depression and lack of motivation, you may find it difficult to find joy in even the most mundane of activities. It's possible that we have a negative attitude on both the world and on ourselves. When we are depressed, not only do our thoughts and emotions become more negative, but we also cease engaging in activities that used to offer us joy.

Our gloomy view can be replaced with one that motivates us to take action if we learn how to do so through cognitive behavioral therapy (also known as CBT). Participating more actively in life has a direct and beneficial impact on our mood as well as our sense of who we are as individuals. The practice of mindfulness can teach us to take our thoughts less seriously, which is another way in which we can further improve our mood. When combined, these strategies have the potential to establish what is known as a "virtuous loop," which is a cycle in which positive changes to our feelings, attitudes, and actions reinforce one another and lead to further positive change.

BE WARNED!

If you are having suicide thoughts or if you think you might be depressed, you should seek help as soon as possible from a therapist or a physician. Even though reading books on self-help might be of tremendous value, we shouldn't rely on them in place of getting prompt medical intervention. You are free to return to this chapter at any time after you have been properly diagnosed and have begun treatment as directed by your medical professional.

Taking Stock

To receive a diagnosis of depression, an individual must exhibit at least five of the following symptoms for a period of at least two weeks before the diagnosis can be made. In addition, according to DSM V, one of these symptoms has to be a loss of pleasure or an overall gloomy mood.

Signs and symptoms:

1. A state of mind that is consistently depressed throughout the day and on most days of the week

2. a decline in interest and pleasure in daily activities, especially hobbies that were formerly enjoyed

3. An unplanned and significant weight loss or gain of at least 5%

4. Difficulty falling asleep or excessive amounts of time spent sleeping

5. Anxiety or the sensation that one is moving at a snail's pace;

6. a decrease in energy and a feeling of weariness

7. Excessive and inappropriate feelings of remorse, as well as ruminating on past transgressions, whether they were genuine or imagined

8. Difficulty concentrating, difficulty making judgments, or difficulty thinking clearly are symptoms you may be experiencing.

9. Ideas of ending one's life, of committing suicide, or of having suicidal tendencies

You are well aware that cognitive behavioral therapy (CBT) is built on the premise that an individual's perspective on the world effects both their emotional state and the actions that they take. Cognitive-behavioral therapy, or CBT, is a strategy that is successful in treating the underlying reasons of this condition by focusing on the following ideas. Different thoughts and beliefs contribute to depressive symptoms, and CBT is an approach that can treat these causes.

Personal Mental Models,

A person's schema consists of their preconceived thoughts and assumptions regarding another person, an object, or a circumstance. We begin to construct mental representations, also known as schemas, of every facet of the event.

There is little doubt that the ambiance, level of service, and selection of dishes offered at each particular eatery will be one-of-a-kind; nonetheless, the principles of operating a prosperous cafe will not change. After a few visits, a restaurant's routine becomes second nature, and you know exactly what to anticipate from your experience there. We may apply our schemas to predict new events and adjust to them, which is why they are of such tremendous assistance to us. They instruct us on how to conduct ourselves with grace and dignity in social circumstances.

You have a "self-schema," much in the same way as you have a "restaurant schema." A belief system is referred to as a self-schema when it determines who a person is and how they should act.

A person who has a healthy self-schema is aware of their flaws but maintains the belief that they are, at their core, kind and kind individuals. On the other hand, sad persons often have negative internal dialogue with themselves.

The following beliefs are indicative of a detrimental self-schema: I can't believe I'm saying this to myself, "I'm just not good enough."

Because of how everyone has abandoned me, I am certain that I will spend the rest of my life feeling isolated and alone. It is hopeless; there is no way that my life will ever amount to anything.

Beck argued that a person's negative self-schema could be formed by traumatic experiences that occurred in their formative years. Imagine a scenario in which a young boy is bullied at school for a number of years. In such a scenario, he can start to believe that the majority of people in society are working against him. If you are consistently hard on yourself, you are putting yourself in a position to experience feelings of depression. If you have a pessimistic outlook on who you are, you won't be able to take the positive things that happen to you in life, such as the satisfaction you get from your relationships, seriously. Even when things are going well, it might be difficult to put one's faith in other people.

Existe-t-il une distinction entre les pensées et les émotions?

There is a distinction, that much is certain. You can think of this in the same way that you would think of a sentence or a statement since thoughts come in structures. Because before to the completion of the concept, you consider a number of different aspects simultaneously in your head, this is the reason why it involves a few different things.

Emotions are distinct from other states because we only need one word to describe them, such as furious or depressed. Consequently, anxiety is experienced as a feeling rather than as a concept by persons who suffer from it. Some of the things that have been going through my thoughts from the past are making me anxious.

Now is the time to concentrate on how we may turn our negative thinking into positive thinking and then maintain that state of mind. We have to let rid of the negative concepts that are occupying space in our heads in order to make place for more positive and truthful ideas.

In this section, we are going to take a look at three different approaches of dealing with our ideas. You may refer to them as the strategies that challenge your thinking.

First tactic: Recognizing and avoiding negative ideas and beliefs.

The second tactic is to locate the pertinent evidence.

The third tactic is to search for a different perspective that is consistent with the evidence.

Now, let's take a look at how each of these tactics operates.

Strategy Number One: Recognizing and Discarding Unproductive Thoughts and Beliefs

We are not accustomed to being able to recall unfavorable thoughts, particularly if they appear out of nowhere and disappear just as quickly. Because of this, it is not always easy to accomplish. In light of this, we need to set aside some time to hone this strategy so that we are prepared to record them whenever they make an appearance. If you find that more than one of your thoughts is upsetting you, you should determine which of those thoughts is the source of the 'bad thought.' When you have it, use a scale that goes from 0 to 100 to determine how strongly you believe in it. The following is a list of questions that you need to ask yourself in order to get an accurate picture of your ideas. You are free to proceed and ask these kinds of questions to stimulate your thinking.

Where are you and what do you see?

What were you doing before you started thinking?

Who else was there during that time?

What were your thoughts at that moment, exactly?

What is the most horrifying thing that has ever crossed your mind?

In the event that it's accurate, what kind of picture does it paint of you?

While you are working on capturing the NATs, there is one thing that you absolutely must keep in mind:

They are presented in the form of brief examples, and they are also specific.

They appear suddenly in the wake of the scenario or incident.

Words and pictures are the primary forms they take.

From a more thoughtful point of view, you do not think that way.

There is no logical progression to the sequence in which they take place.

When you stop to think about it, they could appear to be rational.

Putting a Cap on Your Thoughts

In the process of attempting to record NATs, it is possible to recognize a recurring theme of negative thinking. In the event that you are unfamiliar with cognitive distortions and what they are, the following is a brief explanation of some of the most common types:

This is the location where everything can be described as this or that. There is nothing in between. Either something is done to the best of one's ability, or it is a complete and utter mess. It is also possible to apply to people, in which case you either have complete love for someone or complete hatred for them.

Problems Associated with Being Too Generic

When you notice anything going wrong and you aren't happy about it, you tend to attribute the same negative outcomes to everything else that is similar. It also happens to humans, where if you see someone who is vengeful, you may come to the conclusion that all people who look like him are vindictive.

Adjusting the Focus of Your Thoughts

This occurs when an individual takes a certain circumstance and focuses on the unfavorable aspects of the scenario for an extended period of time. Because of this, you are forced to treat anything that goes wrong as being of similar importance.

Eliminating All of the Positive

In this case, you ignore any true information that could be significant to what you are going through because you consider it unlikely that it will be helpful in some way, shape, or form. In this approach, you maintain a negative mode of thinking that is at odds with the experiences you have on a regular basis.

The Practice of Leaping to Conclusions

It requires choosing unfavorable courses of action despite the absence of unambiguous evidence to back up the conclusions drawn. It also involves strange mind reading in which you get to a conclusion, such as the fact that others are not reacting positively towards you, but you choose not to investigate further into what the problem is. There are instances when it comes down to forecasting that the outcomes of events would be unfavorable and basing your prediction on facts.

The act of catastrophizing

After coming to the conclusion that something is seriously wrong, a person may then begin to exacerbate the core problems associated with the circumstance. That is how you get to the point where you are limiting your achievements or possibilities.

Using one's feelings to guide one's reasoning

You have certain unfavorable feelings, and as a result, you correlate those feelings with the way things appear to you. If you convince yourself that you are unable to accomplish something, you will convince yourself that it is in fact impossible to do so.

Putting Into Action What You Ought To or Have To Do

Taking steps in the direction of setting goals based on what you believe you should be doing. They are frequently lofty and unreachable, despite the amount of effort you put into pushing yourself to get closer to achieving them. If you don't succeed, which is probably what will happen to you given the majority of people's track records, you might feel guilty about it. It can also happen when you use language like "must" and "should" with other people, which ultimately results in you feeling angry and frustrated with those people.

Putting Labels On Things, and Sometimes the Wrong Ones Too

It is a type of generalization that takes things to their logical conclusions. You define yourself as the worst possible person, rather than focusing on the ways in which you fall short. If someone's actions are not appropriate and they irritate you, you can move on by labeling them as "just weird" and moving on with your life. You have a habit of using language that is always loaded with emotions, which is one of the things that contributes to your tendency to attach the incorrect tag.

Personalized treatment

You have the perception that you are the origin of some unfavorable aspect of an event or the origin of the entire unfavorable circumstance. Despite identifying yourself as the primary offender, it is highly likely that you are not even connected in any way to what took place.

The first assignment

Consider the unproductive ways that you tend to think about or that you use to think negatively. Do you observe a recurring theme?

Think About Whether Or Not You Should Speak Out.

Conflict and disagreement are often quite unpleasant experiences. They have an impact on your mood, can set off your stress reactions, and can be detrimental to both your relationships and your career. Typically, they are the result of two opposing viewpoints that are unable to agree on a common ground. For instance, a colleague of yours might want you to approach a problem in a particular manner that you disagree with, a member of your family might disagree with the way that you parent your children, or your partner might have a different idea in regards to how you communicate.

It's possible that you believe that events like this are simply unavoidable at times and that there's nothing you can do to alleviate the tension that they cause.

On the other hand, I'd want to debate you on that point.

What would happen if, the next time anything like this occurred, you made sure to keep any angry thoughts to yourself? Would there be total disintegration of the world? If you did this, how much of your integrity would you lose? No, I don't think so at all. On the other hand, you will relieve a significant amount of stress for yourself.

There are times when these things just do not matter, and expressing them will not either save the world or change it in a way that is more in line with your preferences. It is possible that just maintaining the peace and moving on with life is the best option in many situations.

Consider doing the opposite of what you normally do if you are the type of person who always keeps their opinions to themselves but finds that this behavior causes them stress. If it is something that is genuinely important to you, then you shouldn't be scared to voice your opinion in a calm and collected manner. It's possible that this will turn out to be the best decision you've ever made.

10. Engage in Creative Visualization That Is Uplifting

The majority of successful people, including top athletes, businessmen, and high achievers, use a technique called positive visualization since it is so effective at getting them the results they seek. By visualizing the end result that you want to achieve, you can improve your chances of achieving your most important goals, overcoming any challenges that you may face along the way, and falling in love with the trip that you are taking to get there.

You can also utilize it to improve how you feel about your life and become more resilient in the face of challenges and difficulties that may come your way. The following is how you can personally profit from this:

Practice in Creating a Positive Imagery

The recommended starting point for newcomers is ten minutes, so program an alarm for that amount of time.

Find a place to sit where you won't be disturbed and close your eyes.

Conjure up a mental image of your ideal, stress-free life and keep it in your thoughts. Where do you see yourself now? What would you be doing in that situation? With whom would you rather be? What would your sense of sight, smell, and taste be like? Visualize it in as much detail as you can and really submerge yourself in the experience.

I need you to turn the volume all the way up now. Raise the number of hues, make it more vibrant and active, and really bring it to life in front of your very eyes by doing these things.

Spend some time investigating the image and trying to imagine how it would feel to have it present in your body.

When the alarm sounds, slowly open your eyes and bring your attention back to the here and now.

11. Don't Be Afraid to Ask for Help

There are moments when you simply can't face the world by yourself. There are times when you simply require assistance. There is nothing shameful about acknowledging that you are in need of assistance, whether that assistance is in the form of physical assistance with a chore, such as caring for an aging parent, or mental support in the form of assistance from friends, family, and trained experts. It might be the only way for you to move forward, and it might be the only way for you to overcome that worry and anxiety without it getting any worse than it already is.

At some point or another, everyone needs a friendly ear to listen to them or a shoulder to weep on, so why shouldn't you as well?

12. Consult with a Counselor or Therapist

Do not be reluctant to seek the help of a therapist if you feel that your stress or anxiety is adversely affecting the quality of your life, or if you feel that holistic help is merely masking the symptoms of the underlying issue. A therapist is an experienced individual who has been trained to understand exactly what you are going through. They are also able to provide the unconditional support that will help keep you from sliding into more serious anxiety disorders, depression, or stress-related disorders. Seeing a therapist can help prevent you from developing these conditions in the first place.

13. Restore the Experience of Pleasure

Take some time out of your day to engage in an activity that provides you pleasure, whatever that may be. Instead of filling your day with tasks, take a step back, breathe deeply, and devote some of your time to all of the hobbies and activities that you used to enjoy but gave up when life became too chaotic.

For me, nothing beats a good session of yoga and catching up with some of my dearest friends. What kind of self-care activities can you perform today that will make you feel good?

14. Acquire the Habit of Proper Breathing

Do you feel like your breathing is normal? I mean, are you truly filling your body with pure, unadulterated oxygen, which will nourish both your body and your intellect, by utilising the entirety of your lungs? If you aren't, there's no need to feel ashamed. Now is the time for you to pay attention to the way that you are breathing in order to keep your stress levels from rising and to assist your body in functioning at its optimal level.

Equal Breathing is the best method that you can utilize to get started, and it's called that for a reason. It is fantastic to use before bed (especially if you suffer from insomnia or other sleep issues), and it is also wonderful for those times when you need to be able to concentrate on the task at hand. This is the procedure to follow:
1) Take a full breath in and hold it for the count of four.

2) Exhale gradually throughout the duration of the count of four.

3) Make use of your entire lungs by forcing air into the very bottom and very top of your lungs rather than just into your chest.

4) Calm down and get back to your regular breathing pattern.

To put it simply, that's all there is to it!

You will be able to put an end to your stress, experience greater happiness, and boost your self-confidence as a direct result of utilizing all of these strategies and methods.

But what happens if it's too late to do anything about it? What happens if you find yourself in the middle of a stressful circumstance and are looking for an efficient escape route?

Your stress levels can be reduced and you can finally feel at peace again with the help of a wide variety of treatments, including herbs, supplements, meals, essential oils, and other types of therapies. Follow along with me into the following chapter to learn more about them and how they can be of use to you.

The Primary Distinctions That Can Be Made Between Moods and Emotions

People have a tendency to forget or become confused about the distinction between their emotions and their moods when it comes to coping with the many different emotions that they experience on a daily basis. This is especially true when it comes to dealing with the many different moods that they experience. People have the potential to learn more about themselves and others if they are able to gain an understanding of what emotions are, as well as what moods are, and build a clearer awareness of the differences between the two.

To our good fortune, the differences between moods and emotions, in general, are quite simple to understand. The emotional states of a person are typically referred to as their moods. Unlike emotions, moods can persist for a considerable amount of time, perhaps for as long as a whole day or even two.

When a person is going through one of their moody phases, they often end up feeling as though they are going through distinct stages that are tough to move away from. This is because gloomy periods tend to last for longer periods of time. It might be that a person is under a lot of strain at work or at home, or that they are having issues with their finances, but the periods of unhappiness often feel as though they are brought on by a variety of events.

On the other hand, emotions appear suddenly but pass away just as suddenly as they appeared. People have a tendency to classify their feelings as either positive or negative; however, this is not always accurate. Emotions are also more likely to be generated by an instant occurrence, which can be something that was spoken by another person, something that was seen, or a memory that a person remembers.

Emotions are more likely to be severe than moods, and they also have a greater variety of possible expressions than moods do. This is primarily owing to the fact that there are a great variety of various feelings, but people tend to generalize moods as either being in a good mood or a poor mood.

One other significant distinction that can be made between moods and emotions is the fact that a person's feelings can be influenced by something as insignificant as a fleeting event. On the other hand, because an attitude can persist for such a significant amount of time, it may be difficult to extricate oneself from it. Because different portions of a person can be affected by multiple emotions at the same time, it is also much simpler to transition from one state of mind to another. This is because humans are able to feel more than one emotion at the same time.

The manner in which a person's sentiments influence that person is another important aspect of emotions. The effect that emotions have on a person is intimately tied to the bodily sensations that a person experiences when they are having those feelings. When a person feels anxious, they may feel as though they have butterflies in their stomach, but when a person is angry, their muscles may become tense. Both of these manifestations are examples of muscle tension. The consequences of emotions might be something that is noted about a particular experience, or they can be the aspect of an emotion that causes the most suffering.

The distinction between moods and emotions is not always easy to make, in part because the two states can coexist in the same individual at the same time. Nevertheless, feelings typically take precedence over moods. For instance, even when a person is in a gloomy mood, there is still a chance that they will experience fleeting bouts of contentment and even joy.

In a same vein, even when a person is enjoying themselves and in a good mood, there is always the chance that they will become depressed or enraged at some point in the future. However, it is much more likely that a person's state of mind will end up having an effect on the emotion that they feel. Because of this, the issue at hand is not necessarily one of mood vs emotions; rather, the focus should be on how the two coexist.

It is possible for a person to experience an emotion that is diametrically opposed to their current mood, just as it is possible for emotions and moods to share similarities with one another. When viewed from this angle, a person's feelings are subject to the mood that they find themselves in at any given moment. When people share similar feelings and states of mind, they are more likely to interpret the same cues in their surroundings in the same way. This can cause their thinking to become distorted as a result. For instance, if a person is in a sour mood, it makes it much simpler for other people to erroneously perceive events in a way that will better mirror that person's sour attitude.

Although gaining a grasp of moods and emotions, and more especially, the distinctions that exist between the two, requires a fair bit of time and effort to accomplish, doing so will prove to be useful in the long run. This is due to the fact that when a person is able to see that the frustration or anger they are feeling is not caused by the people around them but rather the mood they were already experiencing before they walked through the door, they find it more reasonable to not blame other people for their bad mood or negative emotions. This is because they are able to see that the frustration or anger they are feeling is not caused by the people around them but rather the mood they were already experiencing before they walked through the door.

The Step-by-Step Guide to Starting a Conversation

Do you ever find that after you've broken the ice by greeting someone, remarking on something, or asking a few questions, you become "tongue-tied"? If you are aware of the critical components at play, maintaining discussions is a piece of cake. Having the appropriate body language, giving the impression that you are interested and curious, as well as being friendly and passionate, are all absolutely necessary. The following are six additional elements to keeping a conversation going in a natural and easy manner.

Pay attention to the circumstances you are now in.
To begin, you are going to identify yourself in the immediate environment, which means you are going to do this right in the room or location where you now are. What brings you to this place? Who else is in this room that you either already know or are interested in getting

to know? What kinds of things are done in this location? How

How did you find yourself at this particular location? What distinguishes this location from others and makes it so interesting? What else can you learn about this location from talking to other people? What are some of the things you did in the past that took place in this location? What are your thoughts regarding this location? You can engage in conversation with other people by only concentrating on the many facets of the present environment you are in. After you have established who you are, it is only natural to wonder what the other people in this location are doing. This strategy can provide a wide variety of subjects for discourse. There is no need for you to consider what to say. Simply take stock of the circumstances at hand and look for a pertinent question or remark to make.

Many people who are not good at conversation have a tendency to focus their attention and thoughts inside rather than on the people and events that are occurring around them. They focus on how they present themselves to others, what those around them may think of them, and whether or not they are liked. They worry about what other people will think of them in terms of their intelligence, attractiveness, and other attributes. These "inward" thoughts will cause you to feel self-conscious and almost completely unconscious of what is taking place around you. Because of this, all of the potential fuel for a conversation that was right in front of your eyes, ears, and nose is now gone. Instead, make use of your senses to observe the finer points of your surroundings and bring them up in conversation. You will feel less self-conscious and uncomfortable if you focus your thoughts and attention outward rather than within. Your level of self-confidence will rise, your fear and feelings of self-doubt will decrease, and you will find that your talks become more natural and continue for longer.

Discover what the other person considers to be their "big" moments in life.

"Hot buttons" are topics that are of keen interest to the people you are conversing with and that build enthusiasm in both yourself and those you are conversing with. If you can locate the truly significant events in a person's life, conversation won't be an issue. These are topics on which either you or your conversational partner may "get into" a deep discussion and continue doing so for a considerable amount of time. Work, a new job, a pastime, a professional goal, an upcoming trip, an athletic activity, a personal dedication to a social cause, and even sex can be considered hot buttons. People's attention might be piqued by a number of different topics and activities. A hot button can be a lifelong interest, a passing fancy, or a current fascination—whatever turns you on! It's essential to find other people's hot buttons as soon as possible because these strong interests are extremely fertile areas for sustained conversations.

You'll have talks that are more energizing and interesting the sooner you see the hot buttons of the other person and the sooner you reveal your own, and you might even find out that you have some strong personal interests in common. Discovering the sensitive areas of another person's personality is one purpose of asking ritual questions. When you are aware of someone's "hot button," you are aware of how to "turn him on," and you also gain insight into the things that person values most highly. You learn what he values by seeing how he spends his resources (time, money, and effort) and how he spends his money. This provides a wealth of material for conversation, as well as enlightening information about the other person you are having the conversation with. Find out what excites someone, but also look for things you have in common with them, such as ideas, experiences, and aspirations. People typically have a wide variety of topics that interest them and that they are eager to discuss. Since we all share common interests, it's important to fish for hot buttons in others. When you find someone with hot buttons similar to yours, you'll be able to find out if he would like to share those activities and interests with you. This is where the beginnings of friendships can be found.

Balance the two-way information exchange.
In a good conversation, the participants are aware of the two-way information exchange passing between them. This information exchange should be a balance between talking and listening. Good Conversation is like playing a game of catch. First, one person has the conversational ball and talks, and then after a bit tosses the Conversation to the other person. This "toss" can be in the form of a question, a request for an opinion, or a comment from the person whose turn it is to talk. Once your partner picks up the conversational ball, he can carry the topic further or change issues. By tossing the conversational ball back and forth, the participants can

balance the sending and receiving of information about one another,

A healthy mix of talking and listening is the key to a satisfying conversation. The participants in a discussion need to be active talkers as well as active listeners for the conversation to be exciting and continue for an extended period of time. Make sure you do both of those things in the Conversation. After you have provided the other person with a condensed version of your thoughts, it is important to make it a point to pass the conversational ball to them. Certain individuals are under the impression that they need to provide extremely detailed justifications for their points of view. In most cases, this is not only needless but also perplexing and even monotonous for your companion. It is best to begin by providing a broad overview of the situation; then, if your spouse is interested in learning more, you can always elaborate with specifics. In order to avoid deviating from the topic at hand, make sure that your questions and comments are centered on the overarching concepts being discussed rather than on irrelevant material. Your audience won't be confused or bored if you do it this way.

Maintain a healthy balance in the information you share. During the time that people are talking to one another, they should be exchanging similar amounts of fundamental personal information, thoughts, opinions, facts, and details. This does not mean that there will be a point-for-point confrontation, but rather that there will be a general equilibrium within the context of the Conversation. You are able to learn about one another at the same pace, gaining familiarity with one another one piece at a time when the information flow is fair. If your conversation is lively, a lot of information will flow back and forth between you, and by the time it's through, each participant will have picked up quite a deal of information about the other. This is a natural way of getting to know individuals, and it will create trust while pushing both parties to give more personal information. Both parties will benefit from this. People who consider themselves "good listeners" may believe that they have no obligation to reveal personal information about themselves and that the information they do reveal is uninteresting and monotonous. They could be under the impression that: "Who gives a damn where I'm from, what I do for a living, or where I went to school?! I'll kill that person with my dull conversation!" It is very important and necessary to be a good listener, but it is also very important and crucial to participate equally in the conversation. The conversation becomes uneven when one party reveals an excessive amount of information while the other participant reveals an insufficient amount of information. Both participants will feel uneasy in the presence of an uneven conversation.

A poor first impression is the natural consequence of having an uneven discourse, which is easy to comprehend. If the flow of information is balanced, containing both real information and small conversation as well as more personal self-disclosures, then the participants will have the impression that they have grown to know each other in a way that is natural and does not pose a threat to them. The more even-handed your conversations are, the quicker you'll get to know the other person, and the better the chances are that your connection will continue to thrive.

After the interview, it's possible that you haven't heard anything in the subsequent day or two. You need not be concerned about this at all. It is very uncommon for the human resources department to take a considerable amount of time before reaching a conclusion, particularly if they are thinking about a large number of potential employees for a position. Nevertheless, you have a number of options available to you for following up in an appropriate manner with the corporation. To get started, consider the following recommendations.

1. Give your subject line a heading that includes a topic that is pertinent to the interview. Say something along these lines: Interview on Friday at 2:00 o'clock. The person conducting the interview or someone from HR will open this email as soon as they see it and will immediately remember the talk that you had with them. After that, you will be able to inquire as to whether or not they

have any information regarding your interview.

2. Give the person your first name as a greeting and bring up the position that you are applying for as well as the tasks that are included in the role. Discuss your previous experiences with the interview process. Please express your gratitude to the interviewer for devoting their time to talking with you.

3. Make it clear that you are still interested in the position and that you see it as being compatible with your own professional and personal aspirations. You should let the person conducting the interview or HR know that you believe you are the best candidate for the job and that you want to be considered further in the process.

4. Make a request for an update on the status of your application. This ought to be brief and get right to the subject. You need to make an inquiry about any available information concerning the results of your profile or interviews. Inquire about the following steps that will be taken throughout the procedure.

5. Before you close up your message, give a brief "thank you" for the person's time and concern.

A Primer On

Sincerely, Rachel

My name is Jason, and on the 10th of January at twelve o'clock I sent my resume and cover letter to _____ Company with hopes of being considered for the position of executive assistant. I wanted to express my gratitude for the opportunity to discuss this role with you. I believe that the requirements for this position are met by my education, experience, and talents, and I am qualified to fill them. I would like to find out the status of my application because I am still enthusiastic about working in this field. Could you please tell me what the next step is in this process, if there is one? When may I expect a response to the application that I submitted?

I am appreciative of both your time and your attention. I hope you enjoy your day.

With best regards,

A. Jason
If you haven't already done so, please send a thank-you note.
You should include a statement that expresses your gratitude and expresses your want to learn more about the status of your application if you have not previously submitted a thank you note. If you have already written a thank you note, you can omit this step.
A Primer On
Dear _____,
I wanted to express my appreciation for the time you spent speaking with me about the _____ position in your organization. The information that was presented was quite informative, and I thought our talk was very enjoyable. I would be grateful for your further consideration as I continue to have an interest in working in this role. I would be very appreciative if you could keep me informed of any developments about my application. I hope you enjoy your day.
With best regards
_____

It is essential to follow up with someone because doing so demonstrates initiative; nevertheless, you should avoid being pushy about anything. You want to show that you are still interested in what is going on, but at the same time, you don't want to appear to be impatient. When you are writing the follow-up emails, demonstrate tolerance and restraint, and don't make unreasonable demands of the interviewer. Take into consideration the length of time required to process a high number of applications and the difficulty involved for an organization in arriving at conclusions regarding who will be hired.

If you have sent an email but have not yet gotten a response, continue to try again.

You should undoubtedly follow up with HR if you have repeatedly emailed them but have not received a response, but you shouldn't give off the impression that you are desperate in doing so. However, you should still send a short email expressing that you have not heard anything yet and that you are interested about the employment. People who show a genuine interest in the process are more likely to get hired by an employer.

A Primer On

Sincerely, Sally

I had the opportunity to be interviewed on _____, and I wanted to follow up on that. It was a wonderful opportunity, and I am very grateful to have had the chance to discuss the role with you. I just wanted to make sure that the last follow-up email that I sent you _____ days ago had been received by you. I am very interested in the possibility of being hired for this role, and I would be grateful if you would continue to take me into consideration for it. Many thanks, and best wishes for a wonderful day.

With warmest regards,

A. James

The final word

It is critical to follow up with HR as soon as feasible after the interview (no later than 24 hours after the interview), as soon as possible after the interview. It's possible that the interviewer won't get back to you right away. You should get ready to wait for it, but you shouldn't allow the opportunity pass you by without taking advantage of it. You still have a shot at getting the job based on how you conduct yourself after the interview. You can successfully increase your chances of being considered for the post by sending a thank-you message and follow-up emails to the interviewer. This will set you apart from other candidates, many of whom are likely applying for more than one position. Because of this, it is really important that you stand out while you are composing these emails, while also demonstrating that you genuinely want the job. If you can convince the interviewers that you have that level of interest in the position, they will remember you throughout the process, and your application will not be thrown into a large pile with the others. Your application, on the other hand, will receive increased attention and consideration from the HR team, which could result in you being offered the job. If you do everything in your power to follow up after the interview, you will demonstrate that you are an excellent candidate and that you are the right person for the position. As a result, you will likely hear some positive news in the near future.

Modify Your Way of Life to Be More Healthful.

Making adjustments to one's way of life can be challenging. People become accustomed to leading their lives in a particular manner, and any alteration to that way of life can make people feel anxious and overpowered. Altering one's way of life, on the other hand, may have a significant ameliorating effect on the lives of depressed individuals who experience depression episodes. The cultivation of helpful and positive connections is one of the most beneficial adjustments that can be made to a person's way of life.

maintaining a consistent schedule for both sleeping and working out.

Putting breathing exercises and relaxation techniques into practice.

Developing more nutritious patterns of eating.

Educating oneself in methods of stress management.

putting an end to erroneous notions and pessimistic thinking.

Developing one's emotional and social capabilities.

You will be able to bring about positive change in numerous facets of your life if you put the above suggestions into action. While it's true that everyone is different, you should make an effort to improve all of these areas to at least some degree because they'll only help you in the long term.

For instance, improving one's diet, sleeping habits, and exercise routine can result in increased levels of energy, an increase in the production of endorphins, and an improvement in one's overall sense of self-image. One other illustration would be the skill of learning to challenge negative thinking. This will help you fight back against the negative ideas that are leading you to spiral deeper into depression. It will also help you recognize that these thoughts are just another symptom of your disease and don't have any real power over you unless you give them that power by giving in to them.

Veronica's Account of It

Veronica was in her mid-twenties when she received her initial diagnosis of serious depression. Even though she was successful in her career and had a fulfilling relationship with her family, she was unable to overcome the void that she felt inside. Over the course of time, these symptoms started to get worse, and Veronica started having more physical problems including chest pains coupled with insomnia and a lack of drive to pursue the things that she was formerly passionate about.

She went to get help after her family strongly urged her to do so, and she has started going to therapy. Veronica did see some improvement as a result of the therapy, but her depression persisted. Although the drug helped to alleviate some of the symptoms, she still did not feel like her usual self even after taking it.

Her counselor eventually suggested that she make some adjustments to both her diet and her workout program. Prior to Veronica's graduation from college, she had a reputation for being quite particular about such matters. On the other hand, when she acquired a job, she had less free time and more responsibilities, so she abandoned that aspect of her life.

Veronica didn't have to wait long before she saw a significant shift in her body once she once again made her physical health a top priority. She began to experience a reduction in the depressive symptoms she had been experiencing, and she began to have more optimistic feelings towards her future prospects. It appeared that Veronica's improvement could be attributed to the integration of nutritional counseling and therapeutic treatment.

Veronica has continued to attend treatment even after some time has passed. She is well aware that in order to preserve her health, she must maintain a state of constant vigilance. She is well aware that if she gives in to her old, destructive habits, she may start a downward spiral. Veronica is adamant that she will not allow it to take place.

Veronica just got engaged a short while ago, and for the first time in a very long time, she is enthusiastic about the possibilities that the future holds for her.

Maintain a balance in your energy.

You are aware of a lump developing in your throat. Either your heart feels as though it skipped a beat, or you get a shiver down to every cell in your body. You are acutely aware of the fact that the energy centers in your body are not aligned with one another. You have a valid point. How do you pull yourself out of this downward spiraling behavior? Simply use your fingers to make contact with the energy chakras located throughout your body. This makes it possible for you to eliminate the actual physical symptoms of anxiety and, at the same time, become more conscious of the natural strength and calmness that your body possesses.

With the help of a potent suggestion, we are going to concentrate on activating four energy centers located throughout your body. The energy chakra located on the crown of your head, also known as chakra number seven, is located at the very top of your head. It is the connection you have to the divine, the spiritual being that resides within you. It is your crown, and while you read about it right now, it may be giving you a tingling sensation. The area in the middle of your forehead is the location of the sixth energy center. Your third eye, also known as your pineal gland, is responsible for transmitting intuitive information to your brain, which you may interpret as a hunch, a premonition, a vision, or a synchronicity that occurs in real life. If you'd like, you can now reach out and touch your third eye. Your neck houses the fifth energy center in your body. Experiencing permission to express oneself is the focus of the third chakra, which is a turquoise blue color. While you do so, lightly touch it and tell it, "I was born lovely. I have earned this. I adore every one of my cells. Regarding affection, the fourth chakra is located in the center of your chest and is known as the heart chakra. Be careful not to hurt it. Observe how it brightens up as your vibration increases now.

This is the course of action that we are going to take. (I want you to read this carefully while you go through a mental rehearsal of it). The following are the stages:

Consider anything that makes you nervous for the second part of this exercise.

2. Determine your current degree of anxiety, with 1 being the lowest and 10 being the highest possible score.

3. When tapping, just use the three fingers in the middle of each hand.

4. Using the middle finger, ring finger, and pinky finger of each hand, tap the crown chakra, which is located at the very top of your head. While doing this, say out loud, "Even though I feel anxious, I love and respect myself."

5. Repetition while tapping the fingers. "I love and respect myself, despite the fact that I experience anxiety."

Tap your pineal gland, which is located in the middle of your forehead, and say to yourself, "I love and respect myself, despite the fact that I experience anxiety."

7. If one is no longer experiencing anxiousness. You just need to say it out loud and tap on it. "I love and respect myself."

8. Place your finger on your neck chakra and say to yourself, "Even though I feel anxious, I still love and respect myself."

9. Tap on your heart chakra and repeat to yourself, "Even though I feel anxiety, I love and respect myself."

10. Sense indigo-purple light tingling through your pineal gland as rainbows of heavenly light encircle your crown chakra and cascade down through it. In the meantime, the transforming blue light that is your voice pours over you like a flood. As you come to the realization that all of your chakras are balancing in the oneness of multi-dimensional light and love, your entire spine begins to light up.

11. When I count to three, you are going to take a FREEZE-FRAME of your energy, allowing all of your senses and the feelings in your body to be captured in that moment. Are you ready? Freeze while I count to three. 1, 2, 3. Keep in

mind that if I say "freeze" with the goal of bringing you back to this state, you will.

How to Break Out of the Cycle of Anxiety

Anxiety is self-perpetuating. When we are in a circumstance that causes us anxiety, such as an interview for a job, and we become aware that we are becoming nervous, we almost immediately begin to become anxious about the fact that we are being anxious. It creates a self-perpetuating loop that has the potential to soon exhaust our capacities for coping.

Because the vast majority of individuals have already been in this catch-22 situation for themselves, I probably do not need to spend much time describing how it feels. The question that needs to be answered is what causes this vicious loop to continue. It is the result of putting two things together. The first step is an awareness that one's anxiety is growing, which then leads to the individual being anxious over their inability to regulate their worry. This cycle repeats itself. However, there is a second component that is not immediately apparent. The second component is the conviction that one needs to be able to keep their anxiousness under control or else something terrible will take place. Having said that, anxiety is perfectly normal. Anxiety can be caused by a variety of circumstances. When we call a certain kind of worry "pathological," we set the expectation for ourselves and others that we should not be nervous. As a consequence of this, the feeling of anxiety serves as evidence that we are unable to live up to these unreasonable expectations. The expectation that we should never feel nervous is manifestly unreasonable, and yet a significant number of people unconsciously place this expectation on themselves.

Altering the Way You Look At It

In instances in which we feel that our anxiety is spiraling out of control, we have two options for managing our anxiety thanks to the explanation that was just given. The term manage is the focus of the previous sentence's analysis.

It would be counterproductive to get rid of the anxiousness. Anxiety is a normal and natural response to everyday stressors, just like breathing is normal and natural. There is no method to get rid of anxiety any more than there is a way to cease breathing. As a result, our objective should be to get it under control to the point that it no longer affects our capacity to carry out our daily activities.

Changing our focus is one of the strategies that can be used to control anxiety. Our concentration on the anxiety is what enables it to grow out of control and spiral out of control. Our ability to pay attention to a number of different things at the same time is severely limited, despite the fact that we are not particularly adept at turning a blind eye to things. The fact that our attentional system has its limits can really work to our advantage when it comes to overcoming worry. If we divert our attention away from the anxiety and toward something else, it will be impossible for us to concentrate on the anxiety that we are experiencing.

What are some of the things that you could concentrate on rather than the anxiety? It is wholly dependant on the activity at hand as well as the circumstances you find yourself in. You should direct your attention to the person conducting the interview as well as the questions they are asking you if you are currently participating in an interview for a job. If you are about to give a talk but are now waiting your turn to speak, you can direct your attention to the individuals who are already giving talks instead of thinking about what you are going to say. If the prospect of driving on a lengthy bridge causes you to feel uncomfortable and you are actually in the process of driving across that bridge, you should focus on the traffic and ensure that there is adequate space between your vehicle and the vehicle in front of you. There isn't really a task for you to concentrate on when you're in a small space like an elevator, but there are a few issues that you should pay attention to instead. Consider the things you have on your to-do list for the later part of the day, for instance.

Again, the goal of this method is to divert your attention away from the source of your fear and onto something else. Concentrate on items that will make your performance better whenever it is possible to do so. You will be really motivated to better your performance, which will make it quite simple for you to keep your attention on what you are doing. If the circumstances do not permit that kind of concentration, the best guideline to follow is to concentrate on things that are already attractive to you in and of themselves. It's possible that you're daydreaming about going on the perfect date with the person of your dreams, but it might also be a list of things you need to get done.

In conclusion, it is necessary to take some time to unwind and do nothing every once in a while. We are not designed to function effectively at all times of the day or night. Only a small percentage of people are even capable of maintaining half of that level of intensity. In order to maintain our mental health, we need to maintain a balance in our lives, and sometimes that means doing things like putting your feet up and reading a trashy novel, binge-watching Netflix, playing golf with pals, or doing absolutely nothing more than taking a nap. The ability to relax is a skill, and anxiety has a tendency to get in the way of the relaxation that we all require. But unwinding is just as essential to your physical and emotional health as maintaining a healthy diet and getting enough sleep every night. Try to relax by engaging in activities that you take pleasure in if you notice that anxiety is making it difficult for you to unwind. You will discover that these activities are effective at capturing your whole attention, so depriving worried thoughts of the energy they need to dominate your attention. This is something that you will find very helpful.

Additional Activities

Other activities, such as taking a warm bath after a long day at work, are also helpful in reducing feelings of worry. You might even use a spa or hot tub instead. When you are anxious, it's a good idea to go somewhere warm and relaxing to calm your nerves down. Even if you only go to a sauna and sit there for around five minutes, you will notice a significant reduction in your anxiety. Warming up your body can help relieve any muscle tension that you might be carrying, which in turn will assist in the reduction of your worry. Even on the chilliest of winter evenings, you may calm your body and mind by making a fire, warming up a cup of tea, and simply sitting there.

Make an effort to move away from the stresses of the house and into an area where you may relax. You should try to rest your thoughts by going to a beach or park, bringing a book with you, and just sitting there for a while. Make an effort not to worry about anything else that is going on in your life right now. You have a responsibility to look after yourself before everyone else. Your health is very important, and having severe anxiety can lead to additional health concerns. Because of this, it is imperative that you take the appropriate actions to relieve yourself of your anxiety as soon as possible. Get away from your stressful situation by hanging out with your pals in a relaxed setting. Every once in a while, you need to get out of the house and spend time in the company of other people.

Move your body.

You can significantly lessen the effects of anxiety by engaging in physical activity. Whether you get up earlier in the morning before you have to go to work and go for a run, or whether you wait until you get home from work and then go for a jog around the block, the important thing is that you get some sort of physical activity every day. When I feel myself beginning to experience nervous feelings, I head to the gym and swim in the pool. My anxiety is much more manageable after a few laps in the pool. Or, if I have anything on my mind and I can't stop thinking about it or worrying about it, I will go for a walk by myself so that I can get my mind off of it.

In addition to this, increasing the amount that you exercise will be beneficial to your sense of self-worth. You will feel better about yourself and get healthier if you participate in physical activity. Get out there and perform some workouts if you are anxious about your health and finding that worrying about it makes your anxiety worse. You don't even have to leave your house; all you have to do is pick a DVD with workouts on it, and you can start getting in shape without ever leaving your living room. It is recommended that whenever you exercise, you do it for at least thirty minutes because this is the optimal amount of time to assist reduce anxiety. According to the findings of several studies, it takes around half an hour for physical activity to begin to reduce levels of anxiety.

If you don't want to work out by yourself, you should recruit a friend to participate in this activity with you. You will feel better as a result of this, and you will also have someone to talk to about the things that are making you anxious. It is wonderful to have someone to whom you can vent all of your emotions and who can also assist you.

Trying to avoid breathing normally

When you first become aware of the symptoms of anxiety creeping up on you, it is a good idea to engage in some breathing exercises. You should try holding your breath by breathing through your nose for three seconds and then exhaling through your mouth. After this, you should try holding your breath for five seconds before exhaling again. To alleviate your anxiousness, repeat this process approximately five times in a succession. If you find that anxiety keeps creeping up on you during the day, make sure to give yourself some time to do the breathing exercises. If you don't feel like performing them in public, you can do them in your vehicle, in the restroom, or in an empty room if you find one and take the time to do these breathing exercises.

Start practising yoga, and see if there are any yoga classes in your area; this is an excellent method for getting rid of anxiety through the practice of breathing techniques. You may also go out and purchase a yoga mat and a DVD so that you can practice yoga in the comfort of your own home. Make an effort to do yoga first thing in the morning and again before you go to bed at night. This will be of great assistance to you in terms of your breathing, and it will also help to relax your nerves, which will result in a reduction in your worry.

Make an effort to participate in an aerobic activity such as jogging, biking, or swimming. These are some excellent examples of various types of workouts that are beneficial to your ability to take deep breaths. If you don't feel like running, you may always stroll or jog instead. Make it a goal to engage in some form of physical activity that allows you to practice the aforementioned breathing techniques while simultaneously providing you with the opportunity to clear your mind of all the pressure and difficulties that your life is currently forcing you to face.

Misconceptions Regarding Ikigai

Because Ikigai can be interpreted in a number of various ways, the core of this time-honored concept is at risk of being misunderstood when translated. Because of this, it is essential to have a clear understanding of what ikigai is and what it is not in order to successfully incorporate the guiding principles of ikigai into your daily life. The following is a list of widespread misconceptions about Ikigai, all of which contribute to an inaccurate understanding of the philosophy:

Ikigai doesn't have to have anything to do with the type of work you perform or the job you have. This is the first myth about ikigai. Ikigai is not about finding something that you are passionate about. Just give it some thought: if the literal translation of ikigai is "the reason for being," then would it be accurate to state that you were destined to work? Although having a job might ensure your financial security and the appropriate job can boost your level of happiness, it is important to remember that your vocation is not the reason you are still here. Only 31% of the 2,000 Japanese men and women who participated in a poll in 2010 characterized their Ikigai as the work that they do (Mitsuhashi, 2017). This finding comes from a study that was carried out in 2010. Therefore, even while a person's job might be deemed their Ikigai, this isn't necessarily the case for everyone. People may find significance in various elements of their lives, such as their families, their health, their adventures, or their contributions to their communities through volunteer work and charitable donations.

Myth 2: Your Ikigai Is Your One and Only Goal in Life

There are others who are of the opinion that your Ikigai is the one and only purpose that you have in this life. This kind of mindset might make it feel like an insurmountable task to find your ikigai. After all, who actually knows where to start when trying to discover their one and only mission in life? If you choose to have one and only one goal for your life, then it stands to reason that you should also give up all of your other interests and devote yourself wholly to pursuing your one and only purpose.

The reality is that your Ikigai can change over time as you develop and acquire new knowledge and skills. Think of it as a unifying principle that you carry throughout your life and that has the potential to emerge in the form of various interests, activities, and objectives as you progress through the various periods of your life. For instance, if you've decided that healing is the overarching concept that guides your life, you might look for careers, hobbies, and life ambitions that incorporate some facet of healing as you develop and advance. Your Ikigai will vary in tandem with both you and the environment that you find yourself in.

Myth 3: In Order to Live My Ikigai, I Need to Either Quit My Job or Start a Business

Ikigai is sometimes mistakenly thought of as a stepping stone on the path to self-employment or freelancing. Because your Ikigai isn't necessarily tied to the job that you do, you don't need to make a career change or lead a nomadic existence in order to live your Ikigai. All you need to do is figure out what it is. You can still fulfill all of your present commitments and responsibilities while simultaneously enhancing the quality of your life in other ways.

Myth 4: Putting the Ikigai Philosophy into Practice Will Only Benefit Oneself

Ikigai is not about putting one's own needs first. In point of fact, there is no more selfless way to go through life than this. When you discover who you are and why you are here, you will be able to make a major difference in the lives of the people around you. You have a heightened awareness of yourself, which makes you more sensitive to the role you play and the responsibilities you have toward your family, community, workplace, and country. Ikigai guides you toward discovering your special niche in the world and zeroing in on the most significant way for you to make a positive impact on the lives of other people.

The fifth myth is that I am either too young or too old to live my ikigai.

At every point in your life, you have the opportunity to discover your Ikigai and put it into practice in a way that is suitable for your stage of development. For instance, the way in which an individual in their late 70s lives their ikigai will seem very different from the way in which a someone in their late 30s or even a teenager lives their ikigai. The philosophical perspective is same throughout all examples; yet, the significance that an individual attaches to their existence is unique to them. It is also true that age is not the ideal benchmark to measure how well a person is living their Ikigai; instead, it is better to assess the amount of fulfillment that they receive as a result of living their Ikigai.